Praise for *A Leader's Guide to Any Situation*

Your book is chock full of wisdom that would be a survival companion to anyone holding a management position in today's uncharted waters. It encourages forward thought by the reader and suggests thinking before acting or measure twice before cutting. It goes back to basic tools from real life situations that worked and worked well. Great Job!!!

T.Pappas, Executive VP, The Speros Companies
Scottsdale, Arizona

Short on pages, long on wisdom.

C. Albright, Technical Engineer
Phoenix, Arizona

An easy read, informative and motivating, especially the chapter on eating an elephant that demystifies and simplifies the planning process for developing a step by step process for moving forward on any project no matter how huge.

D. Brewer, Realtor, CIAS, IRES, CDPE, SFR
Home Smart Realty, Scottsdale, Arizona

The observations and common sense advice from the author's "in the trenches" experience gives us a highly effective perspective on the value of good leadership in any role you may be called upon to meet.

Carl Schneider, USAF (Maj.Gen.Ret.)
Scottsdale, Arizona

Real Leaders Institute, LLC
P.O. Box 2557
Gilbert, Arizona 85299
USA
Telephone: 480-688-0285/602-573-0745
Fax: 480-948-3788
Email: support@RealLeadersInstitute.com

ISBN: 978-0-9762229-2-7

Printed in United States of America
10 9 8 7 6 5 4 3 2 1 0

A Leader's
GUIDE
TO ANY
SITUATION

Also by John Nicholas

You're a Leader - Now What?
Knowing What to Do Next
(co-author)

Dedicated To

My wonderful family for all of their

encouragement and support

"If your actions inspire others to dream more, learn more, do more and become more, you are a leader."

John Quincy Adams
President of The United States
(1825 – 1829)

A Leader's
GUIDE
TO ANY
SITUATION
THE 10 KEY
STRATEGIES

John Nicholas

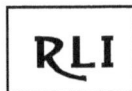

RLI

A Real Leaders Institute Publication

Table of Contents

Introduction: The Biggest Myths of Leadership

THE DEFINITION of *leadership* is as elusive as it is finite. Perhaps this statement attributed to a U.S. Supreme Court justice, presiding over an obscenity case, is most applicable, *"I can't define it, but I know it when I see it."*

Rather than add to the potpourri of definitions, I've attempted to express leadership in this book for you to *SEE* rather than accept academically.

Some leadership writers, with good intentions, tend to perpetuate common myths that have taken hold like a fish hook in the thumb. Eventually, they become accepted wisdom even though, under scrutiny, may not pass the high noon test.

Here are three of the biggest that seem to pervade the landscape of commonly accepted wisdom when, with a little introspection, they actually turn out to be incomplete truths, somewhat misleading and in need of serious clarification.

Myth#1: **Practice makes perfect.**
Reality: **Perfect practice makes perfect.**

You've most likely heard the old story, *"How do you get to Carnegie Hall? Practice! Practice! Practice!"* Leadership is a lot like that, but the practice has to be as perfect as possible.

That means avoiding picking up bad habits here and there. You can practice a sport, a musical instrument or any other skill on your own and get passable results.

But, if you aren't doing it right from the *git-go,* then you may end up perfecting a less than perfect skill!

If that happens and you want to improve, you would then have to unlearn it and start over properly. You must *p-e-r-f-e-c-t* the perfect in order to be good at anything and reap the rewards thereof.

How?

Every top rated professional athlete I know of has a coach. Therefore, learn the right way to do something. How? Seek out a mentor leadership coach. Follow those who are recognized for demonstrating good leadership skills.

In the interim, read and apply good practical leadership strategies from those who have *"been there, done that"* (just as you're doing now).

Myth#2: Knowledge is POWER
Reality: Knowledge APPLIED is POWER

When you have the knowledge but do little with it, it's the same as not having it at all. I once heard the statement; *"Better to know half as much about something, but be able to get it across twice as good as someone with twice your knowledge who doesn't get any of it across."* A mouthful, I know, but you get the idea.

Myth#3: You have to be twice as good as others to get ahead.
Reality: You only need a 1% slight edge (if even that).

The first place Olympic 50 meter free style swimmer gets gold, while the number four gets nothing, zero, zilch, nada (maybe glory). Yet, the difference is often just 10ths of a second. All you need is that slight edge.

Successful leadership is a lot like that. It's better to apply your energy to becoming just

1% better in 100 areas rather than focus it all on becoming 100% better in just one area.

There are many more myths, but by being aware of these **three** you arm yourself to question the validity of all the others. Leaders need to understand the myths of commonly accepted wisdom and temper them with the realities. Are they sufficient to stand alone or do they need some further development to stand the tide of scrutiny?

May you find this book an on-going reference beacon to light your way toward true leadership growth.

John Nicholas

Chapter One

What is a True *Big Picture* Leader?

THE ATTITUDE that to be a good leader you must focus only on the *big picture* and leave all the details to underlings is a recipe for disaster.

How Effective Leaders Do It

Effective leaders have the ability to zero in on a multitude of operational details. This does not mean they become micromanagers involved in the intimate mechanics of every process. What they must know at all times is:

- what needs to be done and by whom,
- if it's happening timely and in proper sequence,
- whether the follow-up system is working.

Seasoned leaders know that no matter how many facts, figures, reports and contingency plans are in place, you can't predict the future. Therefore, you must be sufficiently aware of the details that affect the big picture so that those all important course corrections can be made timely and accurately. This is called *Situational Awareness* or *SA*. Ask any pilot who has ever experienced an emergency.

Attention to Detail

By paying attention to detail you'll be better prepared to make those crucial decisions in a timely manner. In the military that leads to advancement and even battlefield commissions. In business and most other organizations, it leads to job security, better assignments, recognition, increased rewards and yes, advancement.

Here's an example, from a first hand experience, that has withstood the test of time.

We Called Him *Red*

Early in my Navy experience aboard the guided missile cruiser USS Little Rock, CLG-4, (cruisers are named after state capitals) I served under an executive officer, a Commander who had red hair (we called him *Red,* in private, of course), who seemed to be everywhere at once.

He was a WWII survivor of a torpedo attack and was my first true example of serious leadership. After over 40 years I still use many of his methods today that helped me gain the edge. I'll share one special one with you here.

Red would often be seen on deck asking the status of certain machinery and weapons systems. Then you would see him in the engineering spaces checking on the status of a noisy pump.

He was even reputed to have been overheard asking a cook on the crew's mess deck if there was enough sugar in the cookies. From guns to butter, he seemed to be everywhere and aware of everything.

When he saw you he would ask the status of a specific task he had delegated. What always impressed me was his attention to detail. How could he maintain the *big picture* yet still remember such finite details on a guided missile cruiser 610 feet long, with a crew of over 800 and his myriad responsibilities?

Red's Secret

Later, I learned the secret that gave him the edge. He kept a small green pocket notebook (Navy issue, of course) and briefly noted personal things about his officer staff and whatever he had delegated to them. Also, he noted any major systems that needed attention that had to be operational for the ship to carry out its mission. He posted in his notebook daily, reviewed it every morning

7

and then several more times during the day.

I still have mine after more than four decades. It's a tattered relic now. I still review it occasionally with nostalgia and thanks to Commander *Red* for setting the example.

His key was not just the notebook. It was the notebook plus the effort to learn personal things of importance about people he led: are they married, children, special circumstances, talents and major goals. He was always visible and approachable because he regularly circulated, called people by name and knew their challenges, problems and efforts to help maintain a constant state of readiness.

My motivation to get things done immediately was that *Red* would never forget and sure enough would ask me about them. As a result of his *big picture-attention-to-detail* type of leadership our ship was always awarded the battle efficiency *E* and maintained high morale.

Over the years, I've applied that leadership process of attention to detail to my business endeavors. It has been one of the secrets contributing to personal success.

Chapter Two

Successful Leadership is Like Eating an Elephant

LEADERS ARE OFTEN faced with overwhelming tasks that seem like trying to eat an elephant. The SECRET to leadership success in those instances is to apply *Kaizen* with *The Law of the Slight Edge!*

Kaizen is a Japanese term that means the process of continuous, ongoing, small, steady incremental improvements. It's the magic of taking something good and making it great. *The Law of the Slight Edge* is: **You don't have to be twice as good to be twice as successful.**

All it takes to gain the edge is to improve just 1% in many areas (maybe even 100) rather than focus all your energy trying to improve 100% in just one area. Smart leaders approach challenges that way.

A Horse Race Example

Have you ever seen a photo finish horse race? How far is the first horse ahead of the second place finisher? It could be less than an inch. Yet, the prize money to the owner can be twice as much.

In one example the first place horse returned $300,000 to its owner, whereas the second place horse returned $175,000. That's almost twice the return for less than a one inch edge!

What Now?

The question of any daunting leadership challenge facing you, no matter what your field or position is, *"What now?"* This is especially true when you are faced with a massive assignment that requires exemplary leadership skills.

It may seem like trying to eat an elephant. So, how do you dine on an elephant? Answer: with continuous, small, incremental bites.

I do not personally know of anyone, no matter what their position from first time supervisor to CEO, who was suddenly thrust into a major leadership role, who didn't inwardly feel like *"What now?"*

A Personal Example

One of my first experiences as a twenty-something young naval officer came when given a major shipboard assignment. I was suddenly the fearless leader of a deck division in charge of the lives, liberty and pursuit of happiness of 20 men. Add to that the responsibility for millions of dollars of ship's boats, guns and machinery. My reaction (as 40 eyeballs stared at me everyday at morning muster) was, *"What now?"*

That has always been my response many years and numerous major leadership situations later. I've dined on many elephants and so will you.

Learn how now and avoid the indigestion that plagues so many other would-be leaders. Avoid trying to forge ahead in one fell swoop without taking it step by step to digest the challenge.

No matter your position, whenever you are selected for a challenging job or assignment, you will feel the pressure. That's normal. It's how you approach it that counts and determines your leadership abilities.

There's no magic formula, but there is a tried and true approach. Look at it as though you're about to eat an elephant. Daunting, but you can do it by practicing *Kaizen* and put into motion the *Law of the Slight Edge.*

Start by taking one bite at a time staying ahead of the curve with continuous, small, deliberate, incremental improvements.

What it Takes to Succeed

People and organizations who follow the process of continual ongoing improvements across the board in small incremental steps will succeed. You too will succeed as a leader by adopting and adapting this concept.

You will outdistance those who swiftly attempt to take one area and focus their entire attention on that one area at the expense of all the others.

Focus first on the big picture and then prioritize the details of what it will take, in a step by step manner, to accomplish the goal.

Teddy Roosevelt advised that the race goes not to the swift but to those who persevere. One way to persevere is to seek the advice of those who have been there, done that. Read their articles and books. Select those tips and techniques that will help you make small incremental improvements to gain the edge.

How Successful Olympic Champions Do It

In a past Olympic 50 meter freestyle swimming event the number one swimmer was only tenths of a second ahead of the number four. Yet, that's all it took to get the gold. What did number four get?

How did the gold winner do it? He focused on the race mentally and then practiced becoming adept at all the small incremental details of what it would take to win including: stroke, hand position, kick, breathing, flip-turn, start position and even the pre-dive splash of water to acclimate to the pool temperature, to name just a few areas.

Had he focused all attention on training just for the start, to possibly gain a slight advantage at first, would certainly have lost to those who focused on improving, even ever so slightly, all the other areas of swimming.

Conclusion

In leadership, as well as in life, that slight edge, gained by the perseverance of continually making small incremental improvements, is all it takes to eat the elephant. *(This is just a metaphor, I love elephants.)*

Chapter Three

How to Be an Inspirational Leader in 3 Steps

"*LEADERSHIP IS THE CAPACITY to translate vision into reality*" advises Warren Bennis, world renowned authority on leadership. Leaders must be inspired. If a leader is not then his followers won't be either. These 3 steps are vital in translating your vision into reality:

1. Paint a picture.

People love stories. Keep your people inspired and motivated by telling short stories that relate to the work and challenges at hand.

Give examples in descriptive word pictures rather than data, philosophy and long drawn out dissertations. Abraham Lincoln was a master at that. He explained why he was adamant about preserving the Union during the civil war by saying, *"A house divided against itself cannot stand."* Those words have lived on through the years as among his most wise and profound statements.

2. Celebrate the successes of others, no matter how small.

I once read (with all due respect to the author) that the Ritz-Carlton Hotel chain has over 30,000 employees. They have a regular ritual of recognition to give local fame to their employees.

In every Ritz-Carlton, everyday and in every department they have a 15 minute meeting in which anyone has a chance to tell a WOW story. A WOW story is how they went above and beyond normal 5 star services.

Recognition for that gives them local fame among their peers (not to mention maintaining the hotel chain's world-wide reputation). It's a wonderful form of recognition that motivates others to look for opportunities to share WOW stories.

3. Articulate a clear, concise and specific one sentence vision...

...and then support everything it takes to make it happen. That's different than a mission statement which is usually long, convoluted and developed by a committee (and that everyone has to pull out a card to read). A vision statement is a picture of a better future.

An example of one of the most famous is former U.S. President John F. Kennedy's moon landing vision statement. On May 25, 1961 he appeared before a joint session of Congress and challenged them with this clear, concise and specific vision: *"I believe that this nation should commit itself to achieving the goal, before this decade is out, of landing a man on the moon and returning him safely to earth."*

He had many skeptics. However, they became true believers when on July 20, 1969 Apollo 11 Commander Neil Armstrong stepped onto the surface of the moon and then returned safely to earth.

Summary
- Tell short stories that relate to the challenges at hand.
- Celebrate the successes of people no matter how small.
- Create and share your vision being clear, concise and specific.

- Visualize the end result and then work back from there to determine the resources and support it takes to make it a reality.
- By following these simple, yet vital steps, you will become recognized as a truly inspirational leader.

———

Chapter Four

Leaders Never Say These 3 Things

THERE IS AN OLD SAYING, *"Perception is reality."* If you wish to be perceived as a leader you must act like one by never saying these 3 things:

1. *"They didn't get back to me."*

Expecting someone to get back with you stops the action. Sometimes, when you're counting on someone else's help and they don't respond in a timely manner, you'll be faced with a status question for which you may not have a ready answer. That's understandable.

A leader would take the initiative with this better response: *"I will check on that today and contact you before the end of the day with the current status."*

That response is direct, positive and definite. Why? It says you will *"CHECK"* on that *"TODAY."* When do you expect an answer?

How about *"BEFORE THE END OF THE DAY"* (even if it's not the final answer, but just an updated status). That response will earn you the most respect, especially by a superior in a position to evaluate you as a leader.

Important: Avoid the wishy-washy type response of: *"I'll look into it and get back to you."* That may sound the same, but it's far from it. Here's why: *"I'll look into it"* comes across as, *"When I get a chance I'll give it a cursory glance."* What does *"...get back to you"* actually mean? Next week, next month? You'll never be perceived as a leader by responding that way.

2. *"I didn't have time."*

Equally as bad is, *"I was too busy!"* No one likes to feel they are second class and not taken seriously enough to be a priority.

The best way to gain the confidence of others, up and down the line, and create an atmosphere of satisfaction and co-operation is to make them feel important, no matter who they are or what the issue.

A leader would say, **"I was working on another situation that came in** *ahead of you which took a little longer than expected. It's finally resolved. Now you're my priority and I'm going to work with you to resolve your situation and stick to it the same way."*

Then do it!

3. "I thought someone else was taking care of that."

Ideally, you should never put yourself in that position. Excuses indicate a roadblock to action. Always ask questions to keep things moving.

Determine exactly where you are in the situation and go forward from there. Take control. Know what's happening at all times and respond like a confident leader.

If you wish to be perceived as a good leader then you must understand that how you say something is just as important as what you say. That's what will set you apart.

It's that recognition that will help propel you ahead a lot faster than many others not so well informed.

> **"** *Small seemingly insignificant tasks are opportunities to show the size of your leadership character.* **"**

Chapter Five

To Succeed BIG As a Leader
Think *small*

WHEN YOU FEEL you're too important to help in some menial, but necessary task, you're only fooling yourself. If you want to severely lessen your chances to be recognized as a leader just respond with, *"You want me to do what?! Get someone else!"* You will never be exempt from the mundane. The upside is: that's what helps to build character to make you a stronger leader.

It's All a Matter of Attitude

My father used to say, *"Son, no matter what you do in life, whether it's leading men in the military or mopping a floor, if you should die doing it, they should be able to say it was your finest hour."*

As a result, my attitude became, *"Do you want me to chair the meeting or set up the chairs for the meeting?"* I encourage you to adopt that attitude and adapt it to your everyday life. Some call that *"servant leadership."* It worked for me and it will work for you.

It doesn't matter the size of the task. That's not relevant. The question is, *"Does it need to be done?"* Are you the one in a position to do it? If so, get busy. We would all like prestige assignments and jobs, but life *ain't* always cooperative that way.

A few years ago, in an episode of the popular TV program *The Apprentice,* one of the candidates refused to carry out a task she thought was beneath her. Her team lost and she was *"fired"* because of that attitude. When you find yourself in a situation like that, step up and accept the challenge graciously.

Small Tasks Are Often Opportunities in Disguise

People are watching, both up and down the line and they are all in a position to propel your career. But, don't do it for that reason. Do it because it's right. Small seemingly insignificant tasks are opportunities to show the size of your leadership character.

Your servant leader's heart is revealed in little acts, done without fanfare or expectations, which others generally don't think of or wouldn't want to do.

Rick Warren, in his book *The Purpose Driven Life* states, *"Great opportunities often disguise themselves in small tasks. The little things in life determine the big things."* May you have many little tasks that lead to big successes.

———

> **" Use every failure as a stepping stone toward what to do successfully. "**

Chapter Six

Leadership Success is Often Preceded by 99% Failure

DURING AN INTERVIEW, when asked the secret of his leadership success, Soichiro Honda, the founder of Honda Motor Company and one of the most respected business leaders in the world, responded that leadership success is 99% failure.

Learning from failure is part of success. People who always play it safe rarely succeed as leaders. The reason is that their fear of failure is greater than their desire to succeed, no matter what they say. So, they play it safe, never truly growing nor never truly failing - just going sideways in a secure comfort zone that's *good enough.*

Failure is Part of Success

Well, *good enough* is *not* good enough if you want to grow and be a truly successfull leader. Failure is part of success. Show me someone who has no failures and I'll show you the biggest failure around.

The year that Babe Ruth set the record for home runs (which lasted for over three decades) was the year he led the American league in strike outs.

When Thomas Edison was still trying to invent the light bulb a reporter asked him how it felt to have failed 400 times. His response was, *"I didn't fail. I learned 400 ways how not to make a light bulb."* He went ahead anyway failing his way to inventing a successful light bulb, to the benefit of the entire world.

Leadership Courage Defined

Leadership courage does not mean being fearless in all your endeavors. True courage is having fear, but being willing to take the risks anyway. Every aspect of history is rich with examples of those leaders who dealt with their fears, learned from their mistakes, continued to take risks and *failed their way to success.*

Conclusion

If you strive to be a true leader you must do your due diligence, curb your fears, take the risks and move forward. If you fail, be certain you know why, pick yourself up and move on with that valuable experience of what not to do.

Use every failure as a stepping stone toward what to do successfully. That's the true formula for becoming a successful leader. Then, don't stop there.

True leaders never rest on their laurels. They take their experience and continually seek out other challenges. That's what makes them valuable. Remember the famous saying by Winston Churchill:

"Success is not final, failure is not fatal: it is the courage to continue that counts"

> **"** *Leadership and all its rewards still depends on practice, skill, courage, perseverance and it is far from a spectator sport.* **"**

Chapter Seven

Leaders Are Out on the Field Not in the Stands

IN ANCIENT ROME the most popular spectator sport was watching gladiator contests in the Coliseum. This gave the teeming number of spectators a vicarious thrill seeing the risks taken and the skill exhibited by just a few.

Fast forward to modern times and things haven't changed much, just a different arena. Today we enjoy professional sports in much the same way.

Organizations are an arena, far more pervasive than ball parks. It is an arena that offers more opportunity and rewards to far more people and is therefore well worth exploring.

Leadership and all its rewards still depends on practice, skill, courage and perseverance and it is far from a spectator sport.

Leaders Learn by Doing

To become an effective leader requires a certain amount of study. However, if you could become an effective leader just by reading great books you would need go no further than this book (as much as I would like it to be otherwise). Leadership, like any other skill, is about learning by doing.

There is an old Chinese proverb, *"Tell me and I'll forget; show me and I may remember; involve me and I'll understand."*

Leadership is the quintessential involvement skill to develop and it's to your advantage to do so continually. Why? In today's world, if you wish to progress in any type organization you must continually be sharpening your leadership skills.

Job proficiency is no longer enough! Advancement is often a competitive situation. All things being equal the one with the best demonstrated leadership skills usually gets the nod.

Seven Secrets to Leadership Mastery

Where should you start and what should you concentrate on to reach the point of mastery? Get experience from as many different areas as possible. They don't always have to be work related. Here are seven:

1. Seek out a mentor, at work or elsewhere, who has demonstrated successful leadership skills.

2. Join trade or business organizations and take an active role in any area where leadership skills are required.

3. Become active in not for profit organizations by taking on responsible roles where leadership is a challenge because of the nature of the group.

Remember, in those type organizations you have no leverage because all are volunteers. That requires the utmost in leadership and motivational skills.

4. Most importantly: After every leadership type situation practice the drill: *"If I had it to do over, what would I do the same and what would I do differently?"*

While still fresh, rehearse the scenario in your mind and file the answers mentally. Invariably you will again be in similar type situations. You can then draw upon your mental reserves and know confidently what to repeat and what not to repeat.

Training yourself to apply that debriefing method regularly will be the fastest method for gaining leadership experience in the shortest amount of time.

That method is used by the U.S. military after missions and has proven very effective in building leadership skills.

5. Attend leadership workshops and interactive seminars and network with other workshop participants. Take the lead by setting-up an accountability group composed of interested fellow participants to meet regularly to share challenges and experiences.

The environment should be one where you are free to share situations and get honest non-judgmental feedback from everyone. Usually 4-5 is an optimum size.

6. Family provides the ultimate environment because of the closeness of the situations that arise. It is here that you may have to exercise your greatest patience, leadership skills and self management.

This applies to extended family also. Treat it as a blessing that will contribute to the joy of your family life as well as lead to leadership mastery that will help to propel you further in your career path.

7. Invest in your personal library. Books alone are not the total answer (as stated earlier). A better approach is to couple the principles you learn by reading good leadership material and applying them out in the field. That leads to developing the most rounded experience level possible.

All of these have the requirement that you be out in the arena taking part in the action rather than in the stands as a spectator where it's safe, less risky and far less rewarding.

—————

> *" Good leaders know when to hold back and when to go forward... "*

Chapter Eight

Leaders Avoid Pyrrhic Victories

THE TERM "PYRRHIC VICTORY" has its roots in military history. However, it has become analogous in fields such as business, law and politics to describe any struggle in which the victory costs more to win than it's worth and can be ruinous in the end.

The phrase is named after an ancient Greek King Pyrrhus whose army suffered irreplaceable casualties in defeating the Romans in 279 BC during the Pyrrhic War. After the battle, it was reported that Pyrrhus summarized his victory with, *"If we are victorious in one more battle with the Romans, we shall be utterly ruined."*

In the final analysis he had lost the majority of his army as well as principal commanders. There were no others there to draw from.

On the other hand the defeated Romans, who suffered greater losses than Pyrrhus did, had a much larger army and depth of command to draw from. So, their losses did less damage to their war effort than Pyrrhus's losses did to his, yet he was the winner!

The Importance of History

It behooves leaders of today to be students of history. The great philosopher, Santayana, once advised (slightly paraphrased), *"The one who does not remember history is bound to repeat it."*

The benefit of being a student of history is to learn what worked and what didn't. This is vital in order to avoid repeating the mistakes of the past, especially when you can learn from others rather than be counseled by your own scars and bruises.

The Greater Lesson

Our leadership focus here is on the importance of avoiding Pyrrhic victories in which it costs more to succeed than is worthwhile and can be ruinous in the long run.

The greater lesson here is to choose your battles wisely as it's not the battles you seek to win, but the war. The key is sustainability.

Real Life Example

As an example, I had a good friend who was in the shipping business who decided to retire from that, settle down and buy a golf course in a summer mountain resort area of northern Arizona. The course needed upgraded and part of it could be platted into vacation home lots.

He was a bit overextended and decided to raise additional funds by increasing membership and greens fees. Ok, so far. However, he also decided not to honor the privileges extended to those who had previously purchased lifetime memberships.

Those members had paid a hefty fee for that type membership which entitled them to play at substantial discounts and afforded them other privileges as well.

His rationale was that his legal counsel advised him he could do that because, according to the lifetime membership contract, it could be interpreted that a new owner need not honor it.

He asked me my thoughts about his strategy. I asked him who his lifetime members were. He replied that among other notables in the town they included the mayor as well as several town council members.

I strongly cautioned him against tampering with the lifetime members because some of them were vital to the success of his long-range plan. He would need their goodwill and cooperation to carry it out. He followed the advice of counsel instead. Litigation followed. He prevailed.

The Price of Victory

As a result he became a classic example of a Pyrrhic victory. Local business people boycotted him, even though they may not have had lifetime memberships.

The local banker would not consider a loan. The mayor and town council, who controlled building permits and other approvals he sorely needed, were almost non-responsive to his requests.

Soon thereafter, he lost the golf course. It represented a substantial amount of his investment capital and eventually created a financial hardship. It was a big price to pay for winning the battle.

Pick Your Battles Carefully

There is a season for all things and that includes waging battles. Good leaders know when to hold back and when to go forward with courage and fortitude when they must risk time, treasure and energy.

Many who are reading this will have situations in business or other areas in which a strategy is legally correct or in accordance with company policy or some other substantial support plank.

The important thing is to use common sense by projecting the situation through to its conclusion. Determine the ramifications or even the potential unintended consequences of any actions. Then, determine if the results will be substantially beneficial enough to make the effort worthwhile thereby avoiding a Pyrrhic victory.

> **"** *Do your homework
> if you want to be a
> respected and successful
> leader! Prepare for expected
> responses in advance.* **"**

Chapter Nine

How Leaders Handle Disagreements

LEADERS MUST ALWAYS be selling, like it or not. You will invariably be faced with the challenge to make presentations to sell your ideas, programs and projects.

Often there will be someone in your audience who does not necessarily agree with your approach. The way you handle them will help determine how well you will be regarded as a leader.

When my grandson, Chase, was 21, and an aspiring manufacturer's rep, he came to me with a dilemma. It appeared that, while giving his marketing presentation on his product line to professional groups, he almost always had a person who disagreed with him.

Problem: How do you handle that?

Resolution: Do your homework if you want to be a successful and respected leader!

Prepare for expected responses in advance. That will narrow your chances of experiencing a negative response or opinion for which you were not otherwise prepared.

However, even the best preparation may not cover all the bases. When that unexpected response occurs (and it will) then try this two step almost universally applicable approach. It may rescue your credibility and respect:

Step One:
Ask two questions:

1. "Why do you think that?"
After the person responds ask:

2. "What do you mean by that?"
Listen carefully and follow-up using Step Two.

Step Two:
If it appears that this is just one person's opinion, who is trying to assert pseudo expertise, then involve your audience with: ***"That's an interesting approach. I would like to know how many others share that opinion and would like to respond."***

Caveat: Maintain control to keep the discussion from ranging too far afield – what you're trying to determine is if there is consensus. If not, thank the party for their response and move on. If there is consensus or the point is well made and it appears that the person does indeed have advanced expertise, respond with:

"You're obviously an expert at this, but I'm not sure everyone here has your knowledge. Rather than take their time now I would like to meet with you privately after and get your advice. Thank you." Then, proceed as rehearsed and planned for the balance of your presentation.

Summary

Memorize the two questions in Step One above to the point where they are almost automatic. This will prevent you from getting caught short with a deer in the headlights look. It also gives you "think" time while the other person is speaking. But, be careful you don't tune them out entirely for they may have valid points.

Will this work all the time? **No.** Will it work the majority of the time? ***You bet!*** It has worked for me almost magically over the years in so many leadership situations that required persuasion.

Chapter Ten

How to Hire the Right Person for the Right Job

PART OF GOOD LEADERSHIP requires skill in the hiring process. Good leaders know that retention of productive employees affects the bottom line as well as morale and growth.

Recruiting, training and then terminating someone are never desirable. There are many good candidates you could hire. However, even though they may have certain desirable skills, they may not be right for the job at hand. The key is not just to hire the right person, but to hire the right person for the right job.

Taking the time to make the correct hire in the first place is worth all of the effort it takes. The right person in the right job will be productive for years to come. The right person in the wrong job will cause problems, waste time, and expense and send you back to square one again.

Six Steps to Improve Your Retention Rate

Retention is directly related to the hiring process. Therefore, in order to minimize turnover and maximize retention and productivity it is vital to focus on this *Six Step* process:

1. Screening Interview

Quickly weed out those who immediately demonstrate they will not fit. Proceed with those who show a history of previous success and who will commit to becoming an employee candidate.

2. Psychological Profile

If your organization does not have a specific test for the type of job you need to fill, there are many different companies that provide tests for various types of jobs. Use the Internet to locate them. Try the search category *"job psychological tests"* as a starter. Research what's available and then go with the test that you determine fits your situation the best.

3. Reference Checking

This is exactly what it says. There are ethical and legal ways to find out about a candidate's history. The most common ways are by talking to their previous employer, suppliers and past associates, to name just a few. Information is where you get it. Always be discreet about what you learned.

4. Comprehensive Interview

This interview should take from six to eight hours over a one to two week period. It should include, on average, two other interviewers of your choosing in order to form a consensus. Keep in mind that this is really a minimal time investment in the multi-year relationship you hope to build.

Some interviewees may try to hide some of their true feelings initially, but most people will become *"themselves"* over a longer interview period.

This process gives you a truer window on the type of candidate that you really have. Another objective is to try to get to know the candidate as well as possible.

Many people applying for a job may not be prepared to make the effort required for such an intense process. The fact that they will stick it out tells you a lot about them.

This may seem time consuming, especially when added to your already extensive schedule. Always remember that you may be spending as much time with this candidate as you do with your family.

Spending the required time now to get to know the person well enough to predict their success can pay huge dividends down the road for all parties.

5. Family Discussion

If they are married, get a little more insight into the candidate by also interviewing their spouse. This is also an opportunity to sell your company to the spouse to gain support.

Then you can turn them into a proponent for the company and the job. Everyone has those down days when they need a calming, supportive, encouraging influence at home.

6. Expectation Interview

After you determine that this is the candidate you want, it's time to reverse the interview process and begin selling them on yourself and your organization.

When to Discuss Money

This is also when the first serious discussion of money occurs. In many cases, the candidate will already be employed and therefore is subject to a counter offer. It's essential that you get a commitment and that you prepare the candidate for this eventuality. If you've done a good job thus far and are competitive and fair, this should not present a problem.

Summary

Take the time to hire the best, even if it takes six to eight hours over a two week time frame. Go through the *Six Step* process:

1. Screening Interview
2. Psychological Profile
3. Reference Checking
4. Comprehensive Interview
5. Family Discussion
6. Expectation Interview

—————

Acknowledgements

I'M FORTUNATE to have in my family talented children who have been most helpful in the writing and formatting of this book. Although all the chapters evolved from my personal experiences, they were instrumental in what should be the focus.

Daughter Kristin, immersed in the corporate world that is the audience for this type leadership education, understands what makes her generation tick and what would be helpful to them. Her editing and suggestions of what would be of interest showed sound judgment, not to mention her great patience with me.

Son Mark, graphic artist with talent to spare, coupled with his knowledge of desktop publishing, was invaluable in the design and formatting of this book. His advice was especially helpful in the design of the book cover.

Daughter Deborah, independent real estate agent, deals regularly with situations that require taking control and leading the way. Her encouragement and thoughts added that extra that's always needed to make a project, such as this, successful.

Their hugs and laughter made this a joy.

This book took its first steps when wife, Maria, became my focus group reviewing chapters, thoughts and ideas as I went through the creation process, offering initial reactions. Sometimes you can be so close to a situation that it takes someone more objective to keep you grounded.

There are others, such as good friends and associates, Len Fuchs, USMC (Col. Ret.) and Carl Schneider, USAF (Maj. Gen. Ret.), both former aviators and true American heroes, who have served their country honorably and are continual inspirations. They encouraged the completion of this work and that it be short on theory and long on common sense and reality, which they acknowledged it is. I could not ask for better.

Other Leadership Sources by the Author & Associates

Co-Author of **You're a Leader – Now What? Knowing What to do Next.** Available on Amazon.com and the website: www.LeaderNowWhat.com

White paper report: **7 Rules of Leadership You Can Learn From the US Military That can be Applied to Any Organization for Personal Success** by the author. (Excerpts from this report were used by the Pentagon in a leadership program.) For a complimentary digital copy email: support@RealLeadersInstitute.com

Thoughts While Shaving is a site that sends an weekly email with 6 brief leadership common sense thought-provoking quotes (Over 170,000 subscribers over past 15 years, including the senior leadership of the military, Federal, State and local governments). Founded by Len Fuchs, author of **Thoughts While Shaving, Volume I** and co-author of **You're a Leader – Now What? Knowing What to do Next.** Subscribe at: www.ThoughtsWhileShaving.com

By accessing any of the above sites you can be certain we respect your privacy and will not in any way share your name and information.